The Holistic Nutrition Handbook for Women

A Practical Guidebook to Holistic Nutrition, Health, and Healing

Jane Moore

Table of Contents

Contents

Introduction

As a woman do you struggle with good nutrition? Finally, there will be no more struggles. This Practical Nutrition Handbook for Women will bring holistic nutrition into focus.

Your body is a fine tune machine and like any fine piece of machinery it needs to be taken care of. When your body receives the necessary holistic nutrition, it's a thing of beauty. Holistic nutrition heals and feeds your mind, body and soul.

Suddenly, your fatigue disappears and you have endless amounts of energy; your brain fog disappears and your concentration and focus increases; your libido returns; your skin looks healthier and more youthful.

You really are what you eat! Are you ready to feel great and feel years younger? Do you desire to have a sense of balance and well being in your life? Are you looking for a healthier you? Holistic nutrition can do all of these.

This Practical Nutrition Handbook is designed for women by women. By the time you have read this book, you will know what foods can heal the body and what foods can harm the body, you'll understand about the use of food to create balance and how what you eat affects you right at the cellular level. They'll be no corner of your nutrition left unturned.

Your body is your temple – healthy eating equals a healthier, more positive you – you desire that!

Holistic Nutrition

Over millions of years the human body has evolved in an incredible way. As humans evolved they ate what available in their natural world. There were no potato chip trees, no cookie trees and no soda pop creeks. They ate whole foods that were packed with nutrients.

Fast forward to today. We live in a fast paced world that demands a great deal of us and we are focused on convenience and that includes the way we eat. We consume an alarming amount of these highly refined and processed foods, because when hunger strikes, it's easier to hit a 'fast food' joint or grab a pop and a chocolate bar than it is to prepare a nutritious meal. As a result, the heart disease, cancer and diabetes rates are increasing at alarming rates. Obesity has become epidemic, even in children.

Today, any American born has a 1 in 3 chance of developing diabetes during their life, yet approx. 80% of all type 2 diabetes can be eliminated with exercise and dietary changes.

Bottom line – if your grandmother wouldn't recognize a food, don't eat it!

What is Holistic Nutrition

Holistic nutrition is healing using whole foods. But what exactly do whole foods look like? Ironically, over the years, this very basic human need has become complicated and perplexing. Whole foods are complete in their natural state just as nature intended.

Think about an egg, an avocado, or a banana – they have a balance of necessary nutrients. They are not refined or altered in any way. Our body knows how to break these whole foods down and use them to create maximum energy and benefits. These holistic foods should be organic so that there are not chemicals or pesticides added. They should also be seasonal and local whenever possible, to ensure the highest nutritional value.

What is the Connection Between Healing and Holistic Nutrition?

The holistic nutrition philosophy relies on the idea that the planet's health includes the quality of the soil that the food is grown, which links directly to the health of us humans. If the soil that your food is grown in lacks nutrients and is polluted with toxins this will have a negative effect on your body. The evidence clearly shows that food that is grown in healthy organic soil is far more nutritious and beneficial to your body.

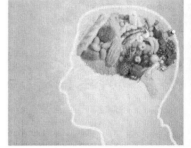

The amazing thing about making sure you eat more whole foods and bringing balance into your life, is that you will almost instantly feel the changes. Symptoms that you didn't even connect with your diet will begin to decrease. For example, are you anxious? Do you have trouble sleeping? The right whole foods can decrease symptoms almost immediately.

As you add more whole and sustaining foods, you will discover that you have less room for refined and processed foods.

The Main Health Benefits Holistic Eating

Food does more than fuel your body, it is also medicine.

"Let food be thy medicine and medicine be thy food."
(Hippocrates)

Some of the main health benefits include:

- Balanced blood sugar levels
- Better sleep
- Chronic illnesses can improve (i.e. obesity, diabetes)
- Constipation relief
- Improved digestion
- Improved mood
- Improved skin tone/texture
- Increased energy
- Preventing disease
- Reduced blood pressure
- Reduced cholesterol
- Strengthened immune system
- Weight loss

Is Holistic Nutrition Right for You?

Food in its natural state is what you and I were meant to eat, yet over the decades convenience has trumped healthy choices. If you find incorporating a diet that is completely holistic is overwhelming, don't worry, because you can start small, with baby steps. Even that will make a significant difference.

You should always talk to your doctor before you make any major changes to your diet or if you plan to use holistic nutrition to reduce the symptoms of a chronic illness.

The 10 Principles of Eating Healthier

The key to holistic nutrition is simple – eat natural, organic, unprocessed foods whenever you can. These 10 principles will help you begin to eat healthier. Pick a handful to incorporate into your day-to-day life or go for it and incorporate all ten. Remember – make changes you can stick with.

1. **Eat whole, raw foods** – This is the most basic principle. Choose foods that are whole, raw and grown locally. For example, a healthy snack might be a banana, grapes, carrots or nuts.

2. **Go organic** – Avoid foods that have been contaminated with hormones, antibiotics, herbicides or pesticides. They are toxic to your body. Organic foods taste much better and they are packed with nutrients.

3. **Get rid of your sweet tooth** – Replace artificial sweeteners, corn syrup and sugar with natural alternatives like honey. Choose naturally sweet fruits rather than cakes, cookies, etc.

4. **Drink enough water** – You've heard this before. Drink 8 glasses of water to promote good digestion. Avoid/eliminate caffeinated beverages, pop and alcohol.
5. **Reduce your salt intake** – Avoid processed foods and don't put the salt shaker on your table.
6. **Buy locally grown produce** – Locally grown produce will taste better and be more nutritious.
7. **Don't eat white flour** – White flour has no nutritional value and it has no fiber. Instead, replace with whole grain choices.
8. **Eat healthy fats** – Healthy fats are necessary for you to enjoy good health. Choose to cook with extra virgin olive oil, coconut oil, grape seed oil, etc. Avoid saturated animal fats, hydrogenated oils and dairy products.
9. **Everything in moderation** – Food is a pleasure we love to enjoy. Don't be afraid to have fun and enjoy what you eat. It's okay to have a meal or snack that's not healthy occasionally. Don't beat yourself up when you do. Remember, everything in moderation.
10. **Watch your portion size** – Portion size is still important, even when you are making healthy food choices, otherwise you can still overeat.

Applying Holistic Nutrition Principles

Holistic medicine deals with your body, mind and spirit. To follow a holistic lifestyle, you should incorporate holistic nutrition principles when you eat.

Here are some tips to help you apply holistic nutrition principles to your day-to-day life.

1. Cut out beverages that are alcoholic or chemical-filled. This includes coffee, sodas, sweetened fruit juices and tea. Instead, drink distilled water, herbal tea and freshly squeezed fruit/vegetable juices.
2. Don't fry your food. Instead grill it or eat it raw.
3. Don't eat foods that contain white flour.
4. Don't eat white rice, only eat brown rice.
5. Eat no more than three ounces of meat a day. Only eat skinless chicken and turkey. Don't eat beef, port, hot dogs, deli meat, etc.
6. Don't eat canned soups. Eat only salt free homemade soups made from beans, vegetables, brown rice and lentils.
7. Don't use seasonings such as salt and pepper or vinegar, other seasonings like onions, garlic and herbs are okay, as is apple cider vinegar.

8. Don't eat sweets made from white/brown sugar, corn syrup, jams and jellies (made with sugar), chocolate or candy (made with sugar). Raw honey, rice syrup and maple syrup are okay to eat.

9. Avoid milk and dairy products made from milk.

10. Eat as much fresh fruit and vegetables as you like. Frozen/canned vegetables are okay, but make sure there has been no sugar/salt added.

Don't eat holistic for a couple of weeks and then go back to eating fried food, fast food and sweets. Deciding to eat holistically is a huge commitment and it is worth the efforts as you begin to reap the rewards.

Understanding Your Digestive Process

There have been complete books written on the subject of digestion, even though this is a science that is still in its infancy

 and not even completely understood by the experts. There is no question that they can be dry and boring to read, yet understanding your digestive process can also be fascinating, and it is so important to understanding the value of holistic nutrition.

We promise not to bore you or make you fall asleep. We'll stick to the basics so that you can apply what you learned to lead a healthier life. We'll look at how your digestive system works and how it might become unbalanced.

Unless you have spent your life being fed by a tube, the reason you are alive today is that your body has the capacity to extract the necessary nutrients from the food that you eat through the digestive process.

The Complexity of Digestion

You might think of digestion in pretty simplistic terms, after all most of us do. You eat something, swallow it, digest it for use within the body, and excrete the waste. Pretty simple right? Wrong!

Digestion is actually fairly complex. It combines biological interactions with chemical reactions the entire trip through your digestive tract. Your digestive tract is split in half. In the upper gastrointestinal tract you have your mouth, esophagus, stomach and duodenum. In your lower gastrointestinal track you have your small intestine and large intestine.

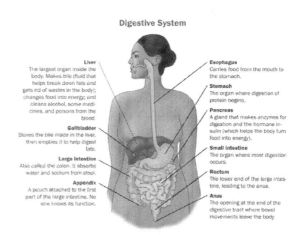

Digestive System

Liver
The largest organ inside the body. Makes bile (fluid that helps break down fats and gets rid of wastes in the body); changes food into energy; and cleans alcohol, some medicines, and poisons from the blood.

Gallbladder
Stores the bile made in the liver, then empties it to help digest fats.

Large Intestine
Also called the colon. It absorbs water and sodium from stool.

Appendix
A pouch attached to the first part of the large intestine. No one knows its function.

Esophagus
Carries food from the mouth to the stomach.

Stomach
The organ where digestion of protein begins.

Pancreas
A gland that makes enzymes for digestion and the hormone insulin (which helps the body turn food into energy).

Small Intestine
The organ where most digestion occurs.

Rectum
The lower end of the large intestine, leading to the anus.

Anus
The opening at the end of the digestive tract where bowel movements leave the body.

What you might not know is that your gastrointestinal tract is also where the largest part of your immune system resides, protecting you from foreign invasion by producing acids and colonies of beneficial bacteria that creates your defense army protecting you from all kinds of pathogens that find their way into your body. So how exactly does your digestive system work? We're going to look at that right now.

It Starts in Your Mouth

Once you choose what you are going to eat, it goes into your mouth and you start to use your teeth and tongue to break down large pieces into small pieces. We call this mastication. Enzymes in our salivary glands start a chemical process of breaking down food so that your body will be able to absorb it, which is why you are supposed to chew your food 20 times.

If you take the time to chew your food you just might surprised at how well you like the taste of what you are eating. Foods are best swallowed when they are at room temperature so let warm foods cool in your mouth and cool foods warm in your mouth. It will help with your digestion.

There is one exception to this rule – that would be water, which is beneficial when taken cold and it does a better job of quenching your thirst.

The first dilemma you face is what it is you are going to eat. Today, there are so many processed foods that are cheap to buy, but the problem is they are loaded with sugar, salt, artificial preservatives, artificial flavors and a host of other chemicals that make these foods more desirable to your taste buds. In addition, the ads promoting these foods never ever tell you that eating them could kill you over time and if it doesn't kill you, it will certainly be detrimental to your health.

There are all kinds of health problems associated with eating processed foods. The majority of people get most of their calories from these highly processed, fast foods. While there are many problems associated with this, there are three key ones you should be aware of.

- Processed foods can cause biological effects that are undesirable. Examples are high fructose corn syrup and trans fats.
- Your body often breaks down these processed foods into toxic molecules. Artificial sweeteners are an excellent example of this.
- Your body could treat these processed foods as foreign invaders and attack them.

When you eat processed foods, you could trigger the release of powerful antibodies that are designed to fight off foreign invaders in your body. This can result in damage to your cells. In fact, if you eat a diet rich in processed or junk food it can cause and internal attack on your digestive system that are ongoing.

This constant internal antibody attack affects each of us differently, and is linked to many of the autoimmune diseases that exist. It can also cause serious damage to body tissue.

The Action in Your Stomach

Once you swallow your food travels past your esophagus and the start of the acid wash in your stomach occurs. A number of problems can occur here. Your stomach is very acidic with a pH 4. It is this acid that provides a defense against harmful pathogens that could slip past the first line of defense. There is protective 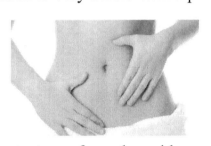 mucous lining in your stomach to protect you from the acid.

These acids are hydrochloric acid and pepsin. When you are younger generally you will adequate acid, so that you properly digest your food. However, as you get older the amount of stomach acid produced is significantly reduced leading to stomach acid problems. It is common for those in their 30s and 40s to experience stomach acid problems because of this drop.

When your stomach acid is compromised, it hinders optimum digestion, and often it will lead to the need for hydrochloric acid or digestive enzymes to be taken.

Anti-Ulcer Drug Dangers

The other so-called digestive aids include proton pump inhibitors, and H2 blockers, which include drugs like Zantac, Prilosec, and Pepsid AC. They will have the opposite effect from what you expect, taking you further away from optimal health. This is because they stop acid production, which makes things worse. So if advertisements have fooled you into thinking that these drugs are helping, you need to know that you are doing your body a great deal of harm long term.

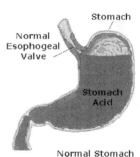

You are reducing stomach acid further and that's already a problem as we age. You the situation with your malfunctioning digestive system even worse. You compromise your vitamin B-12 absorption.

According to the FDA taking these drugs for longer than three 14-day periods is dangerous and risky, because the long-term effects are not yet understood.

The acid reducing drugs are not meant to be a solution for your chronic poor digestion. What's worse is that short term use of acid reducing drugs risk long term side effects:

- **Rash** Dark urine, Yellowing of the eyes or skin
- **Decreased bone density** - Liver disease, unusual bleeding or bruising.
- **Insufficient elimination of pathogenic organisms** - Swelling of the hands, feet or ankles, depression
- **Severe abdominal pain** - Chest pain, vision changes, unusual tiredness
- **Dizziness** –With severe diarrhea

You can see how acid indigestion medications are causing problems. It is actually increasing the stomach acid, not decreasing it.

Ensure Your Vitamin B-12 Levels Are Good

Vitamin B-12 needs plenty of acid to break it down, so it can only be digested when you have high stomach acid content. If you shut down your stomach acid production, your body won't get adequate amounts of B-12 from the food you are eating.

Even an oral B-12 supplementation won't help as it won't break down in your stomach if your acid production is low. In fact, the only way to get adequate amounts is through injections. Let's look at why it's so important for you to get enough B12.

Neurological Symptoms
- Balance issues
- Delusions
- Depression
- Headaches
- Impulse control
- Mental confusion
- Pins and needles in the extremities

Gastrointestinal Symptoms
- Bloating
- Constipation
- Diarrhea
- Loss of appetite
- Nausea

- Vomiting
- Weight loss

Other Symptoms

- Fatigue
- Shortness of breath with only very light exertion
- White spots on the skin from decreased melatonin

It becomes clear that it is important to keep your body's B-12 absorption system functioning properly, because without B-12 you could find yourself dealing with a host of health issues.

The Role of Good Bacteria

As we move further into your digestive tract we reach the small intestine, where there are about 100 trillion microorganisms that 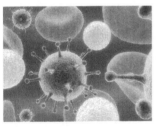 live in your gut. Think about this – that is actually ten times more than the total number of cells you have in your entire body.

They help to break down the food. These yeasts, fungi and bacteria can produce waste products that are actually beneficial.

They feast on the food you are digesting, such as B and K vitamins that your body needs.

They also break down those foods your body is unable to absorb on its own. They change your carbohydrates into usable, simple, sugars and they change proteins into usable amino acids.

However, if you are eating too many sugars, grains, and processed foods, which fertilizer yeast and bad bacteria, it will cause them to multiply rapidly. One of the smartest things you can do for your digestive health is to eliminate sugars and processed foods.

There are an estimated 80 million women suffering from harmful yeast overgrowth. Symptoms of yeast overgrowth include:

- Asthma
- Cancer
- Chronic fatigue
- Depression
- Fibromyalgia
- Food allergies

- Irritable bowel syndrome (IBS)
- Migraines
- PMS
- Vaginitis
- Weight gain
- Yeast infections

It's a long and varied list and the symptoms can mimic other diseases. The key to avoiding yeast infections is to maintain good intestinal health, especially in your small intestine and it keeps an optimum balance of good and bad microorganisms.

Contrary to what you might believe about probiotics not being able to survive the highly acidic wash that is in your stomach, good bacteria like acidophilus will thrive in this environment and create lactic acid to help your stomach maintain a more acidic condition in your small intestine.

Some examples of health problems that you could find yourself dealing with if your microorganisms are out of balance for long periods of time include:

- Bad breath
- Brain fogginess

- Candida yeast overrun
- Chronic fatigue
- Foul gas
- Impaired digestion and absorption
- Lowered immunity
- Toxemia

Some fermented foods that can be very beneficial include:

- Black garlic
- Kefir
- Kimchi
- Lassi
- Miso
- Sauerkraut
- Tempeh

If you aren't able to find the foods that will increase your good bacteria, you can take a quality probiotic supplement.

Chewing Gum and Your Digestive System

You have heard it before. Chewing gum fools your digestive system into thinking you have eaten. But is this true and is it good? Your body activates your digestive process through chewing. It does this because your body needs the enzymes and acid chewing creates to digest your food. However, chewing when you are not eating can be counterproductive.

When you chew gum, physical signals are sent to your digestive system that food is about to enter the system. Enzymes and acids are activated when you chew your gum and these can cause bloating and overproduction of stomach acid. Chewing gum can also cause jaw muscle imbalance and even TMJ, which can be a painful chronic condition.

You should not chew gum or if you do choose gum make sure it's only occasionally or right before a meal so the acid and enzymes stimulated can be utilized.

The Touch Organ – Your Gallbladder

Your gallbladder stores bile, which your liver produces and releases into the digestive tract as it is needed. Sometimes, the gallbladder becomes diseased and surgery is required to remove it. It is much better to address the cause o f your malfunctioning gallbladder than to have surgery to have it removed. This treats only the symptoms and not the underlying problem. Instead, you should address digestive issues at the source of the problem, which is the food you eat.

Occasionally, when gallbladder disease is advanced the removal of the gallbladder cannot be avoided. Without your gallbladder you will have trouble breaking food down in your digestive tract, especially fat, and diarrhea can become a problem. Taking HCL and enzyme can help with the poor digestion that occurs after gallbladder surgery.

Your Digestive System in a Nut Shell

We hope having a look at your digestive system has helped you to a better understanding its role and why it is so important for you to provide your body with the necessary fuel and good digestive aids through the foods you eat.

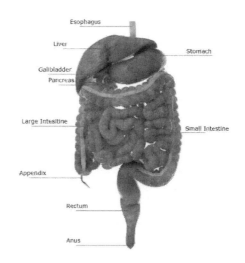

You should also now realize why processed foods and simple sugars are dangerous to your overall health.

Your digestive system is very complex and it has an incredibly strong defense mechanism against invaders. You can give your digestive system a helping hand by:

- Avoiding a diet that is rich in simple sugars
- Avoiding GMO foods
- Avoiding man-made chemicals
- Avoiding pharmaceutical drugs
- Consuming a balance of different types of foods
- Consuming fermented foods
- Consuming foods as close to their natural state as possible
- Consuming raw foods regularly

In today's world, it is really a training act to get your body to recognize whole natural foods as nutritious and delicious, when the alternatives seem to be so much more appealing to your senses. You can and should do it – It's up to you to take care of your digestive system.

Calories

Human ingenuity has figured out how to provide the highest amount of calories as possible in our foods, which means your intestines never have to do much work, nor does the bacteria in your body. Our modern diets are a testament to our

 evolutionary success, or at least our Paleo ancestors who needed excess calories, would think so. However, from a modern perspective, they are actually quite the opposite – a failure.

We now way too many calories in our diet and many of them are low quality calories.

Did you know that right now one in three Americans are obese? Over the last 30 years, not only has the overall number of calories we eat increased, so has the number of calories from highly processed foods. What this means is that we would all be much better off if we ate fewer processed foods and increased the amount of raw foods we ate, because these foods tend to have far more nutrients and at the same time do not jeopardize your calorie count. In fact, if you were to change your diet and eat these raw foods, you could actually lose weight with little effort, while maintaining the exact calories you have been consuming.

However, you must also realize that how much weight you lose depends on the biological  makeup of the plants and animals you eat, in combination with who you and your microbes are – a part of science we are just beginning to explore and understand.

A Holistic Balanced Diet

We hear it all the time – experts emphasizing just how important it is for us to eat a balanced diet to stay healthy. But what does that look like exactly? We are what we eat so it's important to know how to eat a balanced diet.

Why a Holistic Balanced Diet is Important

1. It Will Prevent Diseases/Infections

When you eat a well-balanced diet, it will help your body fight off many diseases/infections. When your body is receiving adequate nutrients, your immune system will function well, which will prevent diabetes, infection, high blood pressure, reduce the risk of chronic diseases like cancer, and heart disease.

2. It Aids in Weight Control

When you eat a balanced diet it will help you maintain your proper weight, and reduce your risk for obesity.

3. Promote Healthy Body Growth

Obtain the essential nutrients to prevent disease and promote fitness. It will also aid your body in growing and maintaining proper function.

4. Aids in Promoting Mental Health

When you eat a well-balanced diet it will help to promote energy boosts, good mental function, enhanced memory, and a reduction in your risk of developing mental disorders.

5. Enhance Your Beauty

Getting the right nutrients promotes your health inside and outside your body - you will look more youthful.

How to Eat a Holistic & Balanced Diet

Fruits and Vegetables

Why it is Important

A diet that includes a variety of fruits and vegetables will provide your body with the necessary vitamins, minerals, and antioxidants. Because they are low in fat and high in water content, they are a good choice for healthy snacks. Research has shown that a balanced diet that is rich in fruits and vegetables will prevent diseases such as heart disease and cancer

How Many Servings Should You Have

Experts recommend that you eat at least five servings of fruits and vegetables per day, and that should include different colors to ensure you receive a variety of nutrients.

Sources

You can eat fruits and vegetables as a snack or incorporate into your smoothies, vegetable soups, salads, juices, or other foods. The best way to eat them is raw, but you can occasionally steam or bake.

Proteins

Why it is Important

Your body needs proteins:

- Grow
- Repair tissue
- Heal injuries

When you lack protein in your diet, it can cause heart problems, muscle deterioration, arthritis, muscle soreness, cramps, loss of sleep, slow wound healing and hair loss.

How Many Servings Should You Have

Experts recommend that as a woman, you have 45 grams of protein daily. If you exercise regularly or you want to build more muscle you may need to increase the amount of protein you eat.

Sources

Foods that are rich in protein include:

- Eggs
- Meat
- Soy products
- Poultry
- Nuts
- Seeds
- Seafood

Animal products are a complete source of all amino acids that promotes growth; however, they also contain high levels of fat. In addition to being a good protein source, oily fish are an excellent source of omega-3 fatty acids, which are important in preventing heart disease. Plant based proteins contain less fat.

Carbohydrates

Why it is Important

Carbohydrates provide you with the energy you need to

function throughout your day. Carbs have fewer calories than proteins and fats and they offer you fiber, which is necessary for you to have a healthy digestive system. Carbs are also rich in antioxidants, which help to prevent heart disease, cancer, and diabetes.

How Many Servings Should You Have

Experts recommend that all of your meals are made up of about one-third carbohydrates.

Sources

Complex carbohydrates from vegetables like legumes, lentils, nuts, potatoes and whole-grains (i.e. brown rice, whole grain pasta) are excellent sources of carbohydrates. However, you should avoid simple carbohydrates or simple sugars like those found in pastries, cakes, snack bars, and chocolate.

Dairy Products

Why it is Important

Dairy foods contain calcium, which is needed to build strong teeth and bones, and to regulate your muscle contractions.

When you do take in enough calcium, you can develop brittle bones and/or osteoporosis.

How Many Servings Should You Have

You should have 3 portions of dairy a day. If you are concerned about your fat intake, just choose low fat dairy options. You can have 1 cup of yogurt, 30 grams of cheese, 200 ml of milk or 250 ml of soya-milk plus calcium.

Sources

Healthful dairy products include:

- Yogurt
- Milk
- Cheese

Butter and cream are very high in fat and should only be used occasionally in moderation. If you are lactose intolerant or vegan you opt for calcium-fortified soy milk and yogurt.

Healthful dairy products include milk, yogurt, cheese, and fromage frais. However, butter and cream must be avoided. Vegans or lactose intolerant individuals can take calcium-fortified soy milk and yogurt.

Dietary Fiber

Why it is Important

A high-fiber diet helps to:

- Control your blood sugar levels
- Lower cholesterol levels
- Maintain a healthy weight
- Normalize bowel movements
- Prevent colorectal cancer
- Promote bowel health

How Many Servings Should You Have

The Institute of Medicine recommends women intake 25 grams of fiber daily and after the age of 50 that amount should be decreased to 21 grams.

Sources

Dietary fiber is found mainly in fruits and vegetables, legumes and whole grains.

Grains

Why it is Important

Eating whole grains as part of your healthy diet will reduce your risk of some diseases such as heart disease, cancer,

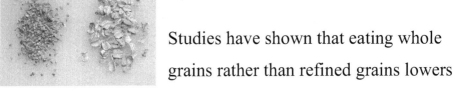 digestive health and type 2 diabetes.

Studies have shown that eating whole grains rather than refined grains lowers your risk of developing many chronic diseases. The maximum benefits are seen with at least 3 servings a day.

Grains are also an excellent source of fiber and will help with weight management.

How Many Servings Should You Have

You should have at least half of their grains as whole grains and you should eat 3 to 5 servings a day.

Sources

Whole grain breads, pastas, cereals, etc. Any grain product that is made using whole grains.

Fats and Oils

Why it is Important

Dietary fat is important for a number of body processes. For example, it fat helps move some of your vitamins around in your body and it also helps make hormones.

There are different types of dietary fat and each affects your blood cholesterol  levels differently. It is important that you replace foods and drinks that are high in saturated and trans fat with ones that are high in polyunsaturated or monounsaturated fats.

Each gram of fat contains twice the kilojoules or energy that proteins or carbohydrates have, which is why if you eat too much dietary fat maintaining your weight could be difficult.

There are four types of fat:

1. **Monounsaturated** - They tend to lower LDL blood cholesterol when they replace saturated fats in the diet.
2. **Polyunsaturated** – They tend to lower LDL blood cholesterol when they replace saturated fats in the diet.

Polyunsaturated fats have a slightly greater impact than monounsaturated fats

3. **Saturated** - Saturated fats contribute to the risk of cardiovascular diseases because they will raise your LDL blood cholesterol levels

4. **Trans fats** - Trans fats act like saturated fats in the body, raising LDL blood cholesterol levels and increasing the risk of cardiovascular diseases and they also lower HDL cholesterol, so they are even more damaging.

How Many Servings Should You Have

The number of fat grams to include in daily diet depends on your total daily calories. The Institute of Medicine of the National Academies recommends that 20 to 35 percent of your daily calories come from healthy fats.

Sources

Saturated fat sources include:

- Butter
- Cheese
- Cream
- Fatty Cuts of Meat
- Full Fat Milk
- Most Commercially Baked Products

Monounsaturated fat sources include:

- Avocado
- Margarine Spreads
- Nut Butters
- Nuts Like Peanuts, Hazelnuts, Cashews And Almonds

Polyunsaturated fat sources:

- Fish
- Nuts Like Brazil Nuts Or Walnuts
- Polyunsaturated Margarines
- Seafood
- Seeds
- Vegetable Oils Like Sunflower, Safflower, Soy And Corn

Trans fat sources:

Naturally found in small amounts in cheese, milk, beef and lamb. In manufactured goods trans fats are found in most baked products.

Omega-3 and Omega-6 Fatty Acids

While part of the fat we need, the omegas are key to our health and we've looked at them on their own.

Why it is Important

Both omega-3 and omega-6 fatty acids are significant components of cell membranes. Omega-3 fatty acids protect against fatal heart disease and have anti-inflammatory qualities, which could play a role in other diseases. Omega-6 fatty acids play a key role in growth, development and brain function.

Other known benefits of Omega 3 and Omega 6 fatty acids include:

- Lower your triglyceride levels
- Reduce blood pressure
- Improve the elasticity of your blood vessels
- Keep your heart rhythm normal
- Thin your blood
- Reduce inflammation
- Support the immune system
- Prevent and treat depression
- Contribute to the development of your frontal brain

How Many Servings Should You Have

Women should have a daily intake of approximately 6 grams a day, with a ratio of 5 grams of Omega-6 to 1 gram of Omega-3.

Omega-6 and Omega-3 Fats sources

- **Omega-6 fats** are primarily found in seeds, nuts and plant oils, like safflower, soy and corn.

- **Omega-3 fats** are found in plant and marine foods, with the latter having the strongest evidence for health benefits. Plant food sources include canola and soy oils. Marine sources include fish, specifically oily fish like mackerel, sardines, Southern blue fin tuna, Atlantic salmon and trevally.

Vitamins in Your Diet

Vitamins are organic substances that are needed for normal cell development, growth and function. There are 13 essential vitamins, and we will look at each.

Fat Soluble Vitamins

Fat soluble vitamins bind to the fat in your stomach. These vitamins are then stored in the body so that they can be used later.

You are far less likely to become deficient in these the fat soluble vitamins A, D, E, and K, but you do need to be careful that you don't build up toxic levels in the body because of over consumption – more is not always better.

Water Soluble Vitamins

The balance of the vitamins are water soluble, which means they can be directly absorbed by the cells. When there are excesses of these vitamins they are flushed out of your system every bathroom break.

Water-soluble vitamins include niacin, biotin, folic acid, pantothenic acid, vitamin C and the four B complex vitamins —

all of these need to be restored more frequently, and your body is able to tolerate higher doses.

Minerals

Minerals are inorganic substances, which means that they do not contain carbon. They are all needed for your body to function normally and to develop. There are macrominerals, which you need in large doses and trace minerals, which you require only tiny doses of.

RDA

RDA or Recommended Dietary Allowances signify the average daily dietary intake of each vitamin and mineral you require in order to stay healthy and nod suffer from deficiencies. These values have been established are based on scientific data by age and gender.

AI or adequate intake level are vitamins that do not yet have an RDA due to lack of scientific data.
UL or upper intake level is the maximum vitamin or mineral dosage that is likely safe for the average person. When you use supplements, you should remain under the UL radar to reduce your risk of toxicity.

The Measurements

Vitamins or minerals that you may need in larger doses are expressed in units of milligrams or mg. Trace minerals and vitamins are expressed in micrograms or mcg. One milligram has 1,000 mcg.

Metabolism

This is the process by which your body converts the food you eat into energy that is used to power everything you do, from thinking to running.

The 13 Key Vitamins

Here are 13 essential vitamins for your bodily function: Vitamins A, C, D, E, K, and B vitamins (riboflavin, niacin, thiamine, foliate, B12, B6, niacin, pantothenic acid and biotin).

Contrary to what you might think, the optimal way to get the vitamins you need is by consuming a varied diet rich in fruits and vegetables, along with other plant foods that include nuts, seeds and whole grains.

There are two types of vitamins- water soluble and fat-soluble vitamins, which we already looked at.

#1 Vitamin A – Retinol

Helps maintain a healthy skeleton, teeth and soft tissue, along with promoting good vision.

Vitamin A is also an important medicine for your immune system. It keeps your skin and mucous membrane cells healthy. Healthy membranes stay moist and resistant to cell damage, inhibiting viruses and bacteria starting an infectious diseases.

Vitamin A Health Benefits:
- Anticancer properties
- Antioxidant properties
- Bone growth
- Bones
- Cardiovascular system
- Cellular health
- Eyes
- Hair
- Immune system
- Membranes
- Mucous linings
- Nails

- Skin
- Teeth
- Vision, night vision, and cataract prevention

What You Need: 2,600 IU or 770 micrograms daily. For lactating women 4,200 IU or 1,300 micrograms.

Foods You Can Get Vitamin A From:
- Cheese
- Eggs
- Fish oil
- Liver
- Meat

#2 Vitamin B1 - Thiamin

Vitamin B1 helps to convert carbohydrates into energy and it is necessary for the functioning of your muscles, nervous system and heart.

Vitamin B1 Health Benefits:
- Act as a mild diuretic properties
- Air sickness, and sea sickness
- Anxiety, stress and depression

- Blood pressure
- Create efficient energy metabolism
- Develop a healthy cardiovascular system
- Digestion, especially carbohydrates
- Growth and development
- Heartburn
- Increase energy production
- Memory and mental clarity
- Mood
- Muscle function
- Nervous system
- Postoperative dental pain
- Relaxation and sleep
- Weight loss and metabolism

What You Need: 10-100 mg of B1. The requirements increase if your diet is high in carbs and/or sugars.

Foods You Can Get Vitamin B1 From:
- Cereals
- Dairy products
- Dried beans
- Fish

- Fortified breads
- Fruits
- Lean meats (especially pork)
- Pasta
- Peas
- Soy beans
- Vegetables
- Whole grains

#3 Vitamin B2 - Riboflavin

B2 or riboflavin is necessary for normal cell growth, function and energy production. Riboflavin converts niacin and B-6 into active forms so the body can use them effectively.

It helps the body produce immune cells to fight infection, and it helps to build red blood cells to transport oxygen to body cells.

Vitamin B2 Health Benefits:
- Antioxidant properties
- Anxiety, stress, and fatigue
- Healthy skin, hair, and nails

- Injuries
- Metabolization of carbohydrates, fats, and proteins for energy
- Migraine headaches
- Nerve-related problems: Numbness & tingling, MS, epilepsy, and Alzheimer's
- Nervous system
- Normal growth and development
- Reproductive system
- Sickle-cell anemia if deficiency in riboflavin
- Skin disorders
- Sore mouth, lips, and tongue
- Vision, eye fatigue, eye lens, and cataract prevention
- Wound healing and after-surgery recovery

It helps other nutrients work as powerful antioxidants, heal wounds, and repair and maintain tissue.

What You Need: 10-400 mg. Higher doses have been shown to reduce migraine headaches.

Foods You Can Get Vitamin B2 From:

- Dairy products
- Eggs
- Fish
- Lean meats
- Legumes
- Milk
- Nuts

#4 Vitamin B3 – Niacin, Nicotinic Acid

Vitamin B3 aids in the functioning of your digestive system, skin, and nerves. It helps to convert food to energy.

Niacin raises HDL and lowers LDL. It promotes circulation by relaxing the blood vessels. It helps keep your brain and nerve cells healthy, and it has anti-inflammatory qualities.

B3 health benefits:
- Arthritis, joint flexibility, and anti-inflammatory effects
- Blood pressure, blood sugar, cholesterol, and triglycerides
- Brain and nerve cells

- Canker sores and bad breath (halitosis)
- Cardiovascular system
- Circulation
- Depression, anxiety, stress, and insomnia
- Diarrhea
- Digestive system and gastrointestinal problems
- Energy metabolization
- Healthy skin
- Migraine headaches
- Nervous system

What You Need: 20 mg a day. Best if taken with other B vitamins. Larger doses can be prescribed by your doctor.

Foods You Can Get Vitamin B2 From:
- Dairy products
- Eggs
- Fish
- Lean meats
- Legumes
- Nuts
- Poultry

#5 Vitamin H - Biotin

Biotins, also known as Vitamin H is essential for growth and metabolism. Vitamin B5 activates the enzymes that are responsible for splitting and rearranging glucose, fatty acid molecules and amino acids.

It plays a key role in energy production and the synthesis of nonessential amino acids and fatty acids. Biotin is involved in the breakdown of fats, proteins, carbohydrates and it helps promote healthy skin, nails and hair.

B5 health benefits:

- Eczema and dermatitis
- Healthy skin, nails, and hair
- Major role in energy production
- Metabolism of carbohydrates, fats, and proteins
- Muscle aches and pains
- Nervous system
- Weak and brittle nails
- Your body's response to insulin and blood sugar levels

What You Need: 300 mcg a day.

Foods You Can Get Vitamin B5 From:

- Eggs

- Fish

- Broccoli

- Cabbage Family Vegetables

- Lean Beef

- Legumes

- Milk And Milk Products

- White And Sweet Potatoes

- Whole Grain Cereals

- Yeast

#6 Vitamin B5 – Pantothenic Acid

B6 is essential for growth and metabolism. Pantothenic Acid, along with Vitamins B1, B2, and B3 work together to make ATP, which is the  fuel your body uses. It activates the adrenals, to release hormones like cortisol, which counteract stress and boost your energy. Pantothenic acid aids in lowering your cholesterol and triglycerides.

B5 health benefits:

- Acne
- Allergies And Nasal Congestion
- Cholesterol And Triglycerides
- Chronic Heartburn And Migraines
- Energy And Athletic Performance
- Healing After Surgery
- Lupus
- Metabolism Of Carbohydrates, Fats, And Proteins
- Nervous System And Stress
- Rheumatoid Arthritis
- Serotonin Production

What You Need: 10-25 mg a day.

Foods You Can Get Vitamin B5 From:

- Broccoli
- Cabbage Family
- Eggs
- Fish
- Lean Beef
- Legumes
- Milk And Milk Products

- Sweet Potatoes
- Vegetables
- White Potatoes
- Whole Grain Cereals
- Yeast

#7 Vitamin B6 - Pyridoxine

B6 is needed for your body to make hemoglobin, for red blood cell metabolism, for your nervous and immune systems to produce antibodies to fight many diseases, and it aids in maintaining the blood sugar level and metabolizing proteins

B6 health benefits:

- Asthma
- Brain neurotransmitters
- Cardiovascular system
- Conversion of tryptophan to niacin
- Depression, anxiety, stress, and insomnia
- Estrogen balance and PMS ailments
- Hand numbness
- Muscle spasms and leg cramps
- Nausea and morning sickness
- Nerve and skin disorders

- Nerve inflammation of carpal tunnel syndrome
- Possible reduction epileptic seizures
- Protein and fat metabolism
- Some neuritis conditions
- Synthesis of anti aging nucleic acids
- The nervous system

What You Need: 2 mg a day.

Foods You Can Get Vitamin B6 From:
- Avocados
- Bananas
- Beans
- Eggs
- Fish
- Legumes
- Meats
- Nuts
- Peanut Butter
- Spinach
- Tomato Juice
- Tuna
- Whole Grains

#8 Vitamin B9 Foliate

Vitamin B9 works with B12 and vitamin C to break down, use and create new proteins. It helps produce DN A, grow tissues and form red blood cells.

Folic Acid is used to build muscle, and heal wounds. It is required for every function in cell division to make sure cells correctly duplicate. It helps produce chemicals for the brain and nervous system.

Folic Acid is also very important in fetal development.

B9 health benefits:

- Cancer prevention of the cervix, lungs, rectum and colon
- Cardiovascular system
- Cholesterol
- Depression and mood
- Gout and irritable bowel syndrome
- Minimize the risk of abnormal pap smears
- Osteoporosis prevention
- Overall good health
- Periodontal disease

What You Need: 400 - 800 mcg a day.

Foods You Can Get Vitamin B9 From:

- Beans
- Citrus fruit
- Dark green leafy vegetables
- Legumes
- Liver
- Pork
- Poultry
- Shell fish
- Whole grains

#9 Vitamin B12 Foliate

Important for metabolism, helps in the formation of red blood cells and in the maintenance of the central nervous system

Vitamin B-12 assists in the metabolism of fatty acids and amino acids that contribute to the formation and maintenance of the nerves, blood, and other cells.

It is essential for cell replication and it plays a critical role in the production of DNA and RNA.

B12 health benefits:

- Regeneration of red blood cells and anemia
- Nervous system
- Depression and anxiety
- Nerve pain, numbness, and tingling
- Proper utilization of fats, carbohydrates, and protein
- Cardiovascular system
- Energy
- Mental agility
- Concentration, and memory
- Possible help with multiple sclerosis and tinnitus
- Growth and development
- Appetite stimulant
- Skin conditions
- Immune system

What You Need: 6 mcg a day.

Foods You Can Get Vitamin B12 From:

- Eggs

- Lamb
- Liver
- Meat
- Milk and milk products.
- Poultry
- Shellfish
- Trout
- Tuna
- Veil
- Yogurt

#10 Vitamin C

Necessary for the growth and repair of tissues, and to form collagen, a protein used to make skin, scar tissue, tendons, ligaments and blood vessels.

BC health benefits:
- Acidity effects for urinary tract infections
- Antioxidant properties
- Cataract prevention
- Cellular health

- Cholesterol
- Collagen formation
- Healthy gums
- Immune system
- Iron absorption
- Laxative effects
- Mild antihistamine properties
- Scurvy
- Viral and bacterial infections

What You Need: 60 mg a day, but dosages up to 2000 mg are considered safe.

Foods You Can Get Vitamin C From:
- Broccoli
- Cantaloupe
- Citrus Fruits
- Green Peppers
- Leafy Greens
- Strawberries
- Sweet Potatoes
- Tomatoes
- Turnip Greens

- White Potatoes

#11 Vitamin D

 Helps the body absorb calcium, regulates the amount of calcium and phosphorus in the blood, and is very important in the prevention of chronic diseases

Vitamin D stimulates the uptake of minerals by bone cells. This process is helpful in building strong bones and healthy teeth.

When there is an excess of Vitamin D in the blood calcium can accumulate in your soft tissues, the kidneys, brain and heart, which can result in seizures, joint pain, disorientation, etc. A Vitamin D deficiency can cause osteomalacia in adults, which causes soft, fragile bones that are porous and break easily. Other symptoms of deficiency include insomnia, diarrhea, nervousness, and muscle twitches.

BC health benefits:
- Absorption of calcium and phosphorus
- Colon, breast, and prostate cancer prevention
- Healthy bones and strong teeth

- Osteoarthritis of the knee
- Rickets in children and osteomalacia in adults

What You Need: 400 IU a day.

Foods You Can Get Vitamin D From:
- Cheese
- Egg Yolks
- Exposure To Sunshine
- Fish Liver Oils
- Herring
- Salmon
- Shrimp
- Small Amounts In Beef Liver
- Tuna

#12 Vitamin E

Vitamin E is an antioxidant and helps to form red blood cells,

protect cell membranes and prevent cancer, heart disease, stroke, reduce bad cholesterol, and prevent blood clots. Vitamin E protects unsaturated fatty acids from being attacked by oxygen and oxidation, to combat the spread of free radicals.

BC health benefits:
- Anticancer properties
- Antioxidant properties
- Blood-thinning effects
- Cardiovascular system
- Cholesterol
- Healthy muscles
- Immune system
- Possible cataract prevention
- Protective effects from cigarette smoke and air pollution
- Skin healing

What You Need: The RDA for Vitamin E is 15-30 IU. Most experts recommend between 400 - 800 IU.

Foods You Can Get Vitamin E From:
- Asparagus
- Corn
- Green leafy vegetables
- Nuts

- Olives
- Seeds
- Spinach
- Wheat germ

#13 Vitamin K

Vitamin K helps your body transport calcium that will be used in bone formation and normal blood clotting. It starts the blood clotting process as soon as a wound occurs.

BC health benefits:

- Cholesterol levels
- Excessive menstrual bleeding
- May help with Crohn's disease and cystic fibrosis
- Morning sickness
- Normal liver functioning
- Osteoporosis
- Radiation therapy support
- Reduction of bleeding after surgery
- Vitality And longevity

What You Need: 65 - 80 mcg.

Foods You Can Get Vitamin D From:

- Alfalfa
- Broccoli,
- Brussels sprouts
- Cabbage
- Canola oil
- Cauliflower
- Fish liver oils
- Green leafy vegetables
- Kale
- Kelp
- Liver
- Olive oil
- Pistachios
- Spinach
- Swiss chard
- Turnip greens

Important Minerals

Calcium

Most of us are know that calcium is necessary for the healthy development of bones and teeth.

However, calcium also plays a role in muscle function, blood pressure, nerve signaling, blood clotting and hormone secretion.

With Vitamin D, calcium can keep osteoporosis at bay. It is rare for you to get too much calcium from your diet, but you can get too much through calcium supplements, which can cause the formation of kidney stone formation and heart disease.

What You Need: 1,000 mg

Ways You Get Calcium:
- Bok Choy
- Cheddar cheese
- Milk
- Rhubarb
- Spinach
- Tofu

- Yogurt

Choline

Choline is a water soluble B vitamin, and it is essential for nerve and brain activities that control memory and muscle

 movement. Choline helps turn the food we eat and our stored energy into fuel.

Vegans, vegetarians, endurance athletes and pregnant women are at higher risk of being choline deficient, which is linked to atherosclerosis, fatty liver disease, neurological disorders, and impaired fetal development.

How to Get It:
- Beef
- Brussels sprouts
- Cooked broccoli
- Eggs
- Milk
- Milk chocolate

Chromium

This trace mineral enhances your insulin activity and the breakdown of the sugars that you eat.

How to Get It:

- Broccoli
- Grape juice
- Whole-wheat products

Copper

Copper is an essential trace element and antioxidant in the creation of red blood cells, and it is also important in the proper immune function, energy metabolism and nervous system.

How to Get It:

- Crabmeat
- Liver
- Nuts
- Oysters
- Raw mushrooms
- Semisweet chocolate

Iodine

Iodine is a crucial part of the thyroid hormones, responsible for maintaining your BMR or basal metabolic rate. Iodine helps to regulate body temperature, muscle and nerve function, and it plays a role in your body's growth and development.

How to Get It:

- Asparagus
- Baked potatoes
- Canned tuna
- Cod
- Milk
- Seaweed
- Shrimp

Iron

Iron helps with hemoglobin, a component of red blood cells,
 and myoglobin, which brings oxygen to your cells. It is important in collagen, amino acid, neurotransmitter and hormone production.

How to Get It:

- Beef
- Cashews
- Lentils
- Oysters
- Potatoes
- Prune juice
- Raisins
- Tofu

Magnesium

Magnesium helps with proper muscle contraction, cell signaling, blood clotting, energy metabolism, building healthy bones and teeth, and blood pressure regulation.

How to Get It:

- Almonds
- Bananas
- Brown rice
- Cooked spinach

- Molasses
- Oat bran

Potassium

Potassium is essential for a steady heartbeat, muscle function

 and the transmission of nervous system signals. It plays a role in balancing fluids by helping your kidney save fluids when we are dehydrated or excreting fluids when there is excess. Potassium is believed to lower blood pressure and benefit your hand and foot bones.

How to Get It:
- Artichokes
- Baked potatoes
- Bananas
- Plums
- Raisins

Sodium Chloride (Salt)

Sodium Chloride is necessary for fluid balance, muscle contractions, digestion, blood pressure

and nerve signal transmission. However, salt is in everything and there is never a problem ensuring adequate salt in your diet as it is present in so many foods.

How to Get It:

- Canned goods
- Hot dogs
- Pickles
- White bread

There are other important minerals that your body uses, but we've touched on the main ones. The key is to make sure you eat a well rounded holistic diet and you'll ensure you get all the vitamins and minerals you need.

What You Need to Know About Sugar

There is no question that sugar gives us an instant 'lift.' In fact, that's one of the reasons why we turn to when we crave comfort and reward.

Even if you don't have a sweet tooth you may could be eating more sugar than you realize especially if you eat processed foods. Everything from cereals to pasta sauce and bread to soups contain sugar.

It's not all doom and gloom – because sugar is a carbohydrate that is found naturally in many foods from lactose in milk to the fructose in fruit. After all, you do need some sugar in your diet. It's what will provide you with your energy to keep your brain active and to fuel your muscles.

The biggest problem is that so many processed foods contain added sugar, which supplies calories but not much else. This means your body has to draw on the nutrients from the rest of your diet to process it and this can have a negative effect, including leaving you at risk of picking up cold and flu bugs.

A high sugar intake will cause your blood sugar levels to shoot up, which will give you that feel-good 'high,' which is followed by you crashing leaving you tired, irritable and with a craving for more sugary foods. It becomes a vicious cycle that can also contribute to weight problems, diabetes and heart disease.

Daily Sugar Allowances

There are two kinds of sugar – that which occurs naturally such as in fruit or the lactose in milk, and that which includes table sugar.

The latest recommendations from the World Health Organization say only 5 percent of your daily calorie intake should consist of added sugars. This is equal to 25grams or about five teaspoons.

Spotting Hidden Sugars

Sugars lurk in the obvious places like soda, but other places might not be so obvious, like the apple you are eating. Let's have a look at some of the places you might find sugars.

- Often low-fat foods or diet foods will contain extra sugar to improve the taste, texture and palatability, as well as add bulk. It is used in place of fat. Ironically, it is worse than fat.

- On average, a can of soda has the equivalent of seven teaspoons of sugar.

- Even savory foods such as sauces and ready made soups contain added sugar.

- The natural sugar in some fruit, including some of the newer varieties of apples, has increased to satisfy the desire for more sweetness.

Read the Label

There is an easy way to find out how much sugar is in a product – read the label.

- When you are reading the nutrition panel look at 'carbs as sugars' - this includes both natural and added sugars. If there is under 5 grams per 100 grams this is low, but if there is more than 15 grams per 100 grams this is high.

- Check the ingredients list for anything that ends in 'ose' (sucrose, glucose, lactose, fructose, maltose), which are all forms of sugar. Agave, honey, molasses and syrups like rice or corn syrup are also sugars. The closer to the top of the ingredients list, the more sugar the product contains.

- Know what sugar substitutes are used. For example, mannitol, xylitol, and sorbitol are sugar substitutes. These naturally occur in small amounts in plants and fruits and they are often used in low-calorie products to provide sweetness, but they have fewer calories than table sugar. Xylitol is used in home-baking as a replacement for regular sugar (ratio 1:1).

How to Cut Down Your Sugar Use

Making just a handful of adjustments to your diet will help you to cut down on needless sugar consumption:

- Reduce the amount of sugar you add to hot drinks. Wean yourself gradually to give your taste buds a chance to adjust. Try adding a sprinkle of cinnamon to your hot chocolate or cappuccino. Cinnamon helps stabilize blood sugar levels and it adds flavor without the sweetness.

- Avoid low-fat 'diet' foods because they often are high in sugars. A better option is to eat smaller portions of the regular versions.

- Be skeptical of 'sugar-free' foods. Far too often these foods contain synthetic sweeteners like saccharin, aspartame or sucralose. Although these artificial sweeteners taste sweet, they won't help curb your sweet tooth, which results in your brain receiving confusing messages. This can lead to over-eating.

- Swap white bread, pasta and rice for whole grain versions like oats, granary and whole meal breads, brown rice and pasta.

- Balance your carb intake with lean protein like chicken, turkey and fish - protein foods slow the emptying of your stomach, which helps manage cravings.

- Have no more than one glass of fruit juice a day and keep save sodas and alcohol for the weekends. Try herbal teas or water with citrus fruit slices.

- Reduce the sugar in your recipes and substitute spices to boost the flavor and taste.

- If you need a pick me up, eat a piece of whole fruit with a handful of nuts or a yogurt. All of these contain protein that will help balance your blood sugar and energy levels.

Cooked vs. Raw

Cooked vs. raw – you have probably heard all kinds of information, so much that it becomes confusing. Well, let's take a minute to look at both the pros and cons of each so that you are better equipped to make your own decisions.

 What does the healthiest diet look like? This is a question that is asked over and over again and it seldom gets the same answer.

That's because if we are being honest, there is no single correct answer.

One approach that's growing quickly in popularity is the raw food diet, where you stick to a routine of strictly uncooked food. There are people that are for and against the raw food diet, which is why it is so important for you to have all of the facts before you take on a 100 percent raw food diet.

Let's look at the pros and cons.

What the Raw Food Diet Promises

Those that support a raw food diet say that raw foods contain natural enzymes along with numerous other nutrients that are broken down during the cooking process. These enzymes are able to improve your digestion and

help you to absorb other beneficial nutrients.

The Difficulties With Raw Food

The raw food theory is certainly plausible, it does go against what traditional Chinese and Ayurvedic teachings follow that believe the nutrients from cooked food are easier to digest, because cooking breaks them down into smaller components, which supports your digestive fire, a warmth and movement that brings vitality to the digestive tract and maintains your overall health.

Raw Foods Are Cool

Raw food diets are more popular in the warmer climates, which makes sense, since traditional Chinese medicine says that raw foods have a cooling effect on the body. If you have a lot of inflammation or heat, you could find balance and greater vitality with a raw food diet. On the other hand, if you frequently feel cold you could become weaker on a long-term raw food program.

What Cooking Food Promises

There are some nutrients that become more available once they are heated. Lycopene is an example of an antioxidant that is found in tomatoes as well as other foods, and the lycopene is more available when these foods are cooked.

Vegetables like spinach, kale, garlic and onions have also been shown to be more nutritious when lightly cooked, which releases compounds that otherwise go undigested.

Overcooking foods, especially meats, produce chemicals that add to inflammation and are linked to some cancers. Lightly steaming or sautéing at moderate temperatures is a great option. It helps to make the nutrients available without producing the harmful by-products of overcooking.

Is Cooked Food Superior to Raw?

Many experts would agree you can't go wrong, striving to eat as much raw food as possible. Ancient humans largely ate a plant-based raw food diet. They may have even occasionally

eaten raw meat. However, when you restrict your foods to only raw plant foods you will likely see a decline in your health over the long term.

Eating as much as 85 percent of your food raw is perfectly safe. Even when ancient humans began to cook their meals, they still ate significantly more raw foods than people do today.

As we already mentioned, there are times when cooking does release more nutrition; however, for the most part cooking your food, especially if it is at a high temperature will destroy enzymes, which speed up and make possible reactions in your body.

In fact, there are actually biochemical reactions that can't happen without these enzymes. That means if you cook all your food, your body is going to be deficient in some and it will also be lacking biophotons.

Living raw foods contain biophoton light energy, which your body needs. Every living organism emits biophotons and it's believed that the higher the level of light energy emitted by a cell, the greater its vitality and the greater the potential that this energy will be transferred to you when you eat it. The more light a food can store, the more nutritious it is.

Grown fresh raw vegetables are rich in light energy. Therefore the capacity to store biophotons is a measure of the food quality.

The greater your store of light energy from healthy raw foods, the greater the power of your overall electromagnetic field, and the more energy you will have available for healing and maintaining your optimal health.

The Cooked Diet of Today is Not Like the Ancient Cooked Diet

Today, most of the cooked foods we eat are in form that is highly processed. In fact, you might be shocked to learn that 90 percent of foods Americans purchase annually are processed foods, and in the form of carbohydrates like grains, fructose, sugar, etc.

These foods are lacking any nutrition, and in addition, the fructose and dietary carbohydrates lead to excess body fat, obesity and other health issues. In ancient times, these were not  the type of cooked foods that were consumed, so even though the ancients may have cooked some of their food it was still primarily in an unprocessed form. After all, there was no such thing as processed foods.

There is a growing belief that eating foods that are consistent with your genetic ancestry can help you to avoid many of the diseases that are linked with the modern diet of today. That includes diseases like heart disease, cancer and diabetes. This is the Paleo Diet, which primarily focuses on a wide variety of raw, whole fruits, vegetables, roots, nuts and meat.

For Many Eating an Ancient Diet Would be an Improvement

Modern humans face all kinds of modern diseases and conditions that our ancestors never ever saw or were rarely seen. Heart disease, cancer, obesity, diabetes... all of these are good examples of modern day health issues. It's apparent that we have strayed too far from the foods that are bodies were designed to eat, so it makes sense that going back to basics and focusing on fresh, whole, unprocessed real food is going to lead to a healthier you.

Generally speaking a "healthy diet" will follow these main factors:

- Eating unprocessed whole foods.
- Eating raw often or only lightly cooked foods. Try to eat at least one-third of your food raw.
- Pastured organic or grass-fed, free from additives and not genetically modified ingredients.
- Come from local, high quality sources.
- Carbohydrates from high-nutrient vegetables, except avoid corn and potatoes.

Balance Is the Answer

There are many benefits to eating large amounts of fresh produce, but there's also a need for cooked foods. The answer really lies in creating balance in your life. A balanced approach will help you get the nutrients you need to maintain overall health, vitality and clarity.

There is no single diet that offers a magical formula for you to enjoy vibrant health. There is no single diet that works for everyone.

While raw foods might be ideal if you have weak digestion, such a diet can be significant for others. A holistic diet does not mean that you eat a 100 percent raw food diet. That's simply not the right choice for everyone.

Over time, a 100 percent raw food diet can put undue stress on your digestive system and actually cause weakness in some people. While the fresh produce abundance is definitely beneficial, most of us need a balance between cooked and raw foods to enjoy optimum vitality long term.

Healthy Cooking

If you are ready for a little guidance on healthy cooking, these 10 principles will get you started in the right direction.

1. **Use Smart Fats** – Not all fat is bad. Opt to use unsaturated fats like olive oil rather than saturated fats like butter.

2. **Go Unrefined** – Choose grains that are whole grains rather than refined grains. For example, choose brown rice rather than white rice.

3. **Increase your fruits and vegetables** – Most people don't get enough fruits and vegetables. You should aim for 4-13 services a day. Pick a variety of colors to get the most antioxidants.

4. **Choose Low Fat Dairy** – Dairy products are a great source of calcium. A healthier choice is to choose low fat options.

5. **Different Meat Choices**– Meat is a good source of protein, but it also is a big source of saturated fat, so opt for lean fish and poultry for a healthier choice.

6. **Watch your Portion Size** – Make sure that you keep your portion size reasonable.

7. **Avoid Sweeteners** – This means all kinds of sweeteners both sugar substitutes and natural, so white sugar, honey, brown sugar and maple syrup.

8. **Reduce Your Sodium** – The recommended guideline says 2,300 mg of salt daily.
9. **Enjoy the Flavor** – Enhance the flavor of your food using natural herbs, citrus and spices.
10. **Enjoy What you Eat** – Make a conscious decision to take the time to enjoy the food you are eating.

Healthy Preparation Methods

- Stock up on heart-healthy cookbooks
- Use choice grades of beef rather than prime and trim off the fat before cooking
- Use loin or round cuts of red meat and pork as they generally have the least fat
- With poultry use the leaner light meat like the breasts rather than the fattier dark meat like the legs and thighs, and remove the skin
- Make egg dishes using egg whites rather than egg yolks
- For recipes using dairy products, choose low-fat or fat-free versions
- Use low fat or no fat salad dressings
- Use and prepare foods with little or no salt.

Smart Substitutions for Healthy Cooking

You can make many of your favorite recipes healthier just by using low or no fat ingredients.

Healthy substitutions can help you cut down on saturated fats, cholesterol and trans fats

Recipe Calls For	Substitute This
Whole milk (1 cup)	1 cup fat-free or low-fat milk, plus one tablespoon of vegetable oil
Heavy cream (1 cup)	1 cup evaporated skim milk or 1/2 cup low-fat yogurt and 1/2 cup plain low-fat unsalted cottage cheese
Sour cream	Low-fat unsalted cottage cheese plus low-fat or fat-free yogurt; or use a fat-free sour cream
Cream cheese	4 tablespoons soft margarine blended with 1 cup dry, unsalted low-fat cottage cheese; then add a small amount of fat-free milk.
Butter (1 tablespoon)	1 tablespoon soft margarine or 3/4 tablespoons liquid vegetable oil
Egg (1)	2 egg whites
Unsweetened baking chocolate (1 ounce)	3 tablespoons unsweetened cocoa powder or carob powder plus 1 tablespoon vegetable oil.

Healthy Snacking

Do you feel guilty when you snack? Well, there's no need to

 feel guilty, nor do you have to stop having your snacks. The key is moderation and healthy snack choices. We broke snacks into four categories, crunchy, thirst quenchers, munchy and sweet so you can find a healthy treat in each category.

Crunchy Treats:

- Apples and breadsticks
- Broccoli spears
- Carrot and celery sticks
- Cauliflower
- Green pepper sticks
- Radishes
- Zucchini circles
- Unsalted rice cakes

Thirst Quenchers:

- Fat-free milk
- Low-sodium tomato
- Mixed vegetable juice
- Unsweetened juices
- Water

Munchy:

- Bagels
- Cherry or grape tomatoes
- Low-fat or fat-free cheese
- Plain, fat free or low-fat yogurt
- Unsalted sunflower seeds
- Whole-grain breads or toast
- Unsalted almonds, walnuts, other nuts

Sweet

- Baked apple
- Dried fruit gelatin gems
- Fresh fruit
- Frozen bananas
- Frozen grapes
- Low-fat or fat-free unsweetened fruit yogurt
- Raisins
- Thin slice of angel food cake
- Unsweetened canned fruit

That's just a few snacks that you can have without feeling guilty. Don't be afraid to think outside the box.

Great, so now that we've looked at raw food and cooked food, along with the pros and cons of each, it's time to move on.

How to Detox Your Body

If you feel sluggish, you find yourself dealing with aches and pains, you have digestive issues, or you just can't lose the weight, a detox is a good idea.

Around the world detoxifying has been practiced for centuries and is a part of Chinese and Ayurvedic medicine systems. When you detox you rest, clean and nourish your body from the inside out. It eliminates and removes toxins, while feeding your body healthy nutrients.

How Detoxification Works

When you detox you clean your blood. This is done by removing the impurities from the blood in the liver, which is where toxins are eliminated from your body. The body also eliminates toxins through your lungs, intestines, lymph, kidneys and skin. However, if your system is compromised by toxins, impurities will not be filtered out properly and this can have adverse effects on you.

The Benefits of Cleansing

The Natural cleansing process will:

1. Rest your organs through fasting

2. Stimulate the liver to drive toxins from the body

3. Promote elimination through the skin, intestines and kidneys

4. Improve circulation of the blood

5. Refuel the body with healthy nutrients.

According to the experts detoxification works because the needs of the individual cell are addressed.

When to Detoxify

You should detox at least once a year unless you are a nursing mother or have cancer, TB, or chronic degenerative diseases. You should always talk to your health care practitioner before you detox.

Signs that you need to detox include:

- Allergies
- Bloating
- Irritated skin
- Low-grade infections
- Menstrual problems
- Mental confusion

- Puffy eye or bags under the eyes

- Sluggish elimination

- Unexplained fatigue

Choosing the Right Detox Program for You

There are several different detoxification programs, so it's best to choose one that directly meets your needs. Many programs use a 7 to 10 day schedule because it takes some time for your body to cleanse the blood. Detoxing involves fasting on liquids for a specific period of time, followed by the detox part of

the program. Here are 5 popular types of detox programs. Later on we will look at a Juicing cleanse.

1. Juice Cleanse
2. Simple Fruit and Veggie Detox
3. Smoothie Cleanse
4. Hypoallergenic Detox
5. Sugar Detox

8 Ways to Aid Your Body in Detoxifying

After you have completed a detox program you can start to take better care of your body by cleansing it daily through your diet, supplements and your lifestyle choices. Let's look at 8 things you can do.

1. Taking herbs like burdock, dandelion root or milk thistle, and drinking green tea to cleanse and protect your liver.
2. Eat plenty of fiber that includes fresh organic fruits and vegetables, like radishes, beets, artichokes, broccoli, spirulina, cabbage, and seaweed which are all terrific detox foods.
3. Take vitamin C daily as it will help the body produce glutathione, which is a liver compound that will drive away toxins.
4. Drink a minimum of two quarts of water a day.
5. Transform stress by emphasizing positive emotions. Learn to breathe deeply so that the oxygen can more completely circulate through your system.
6. Practice hydrotherapy by taking a 5 minute very hot shower, and letting the water run down your back. Then follow with a 30 second cold water shower. Repeat 3 times, and then get into bed for 30 minutes.
7. Dry-brush your skin to remove toxins through your pores.

8. Sweat in a sauna so your body can eliminate waste by perspiring.

Juicing

Deciding to juice is a big decision and it's a good decision. There are many benefits and it is something you can do throughout the year.

Juicing allows you get those micronutrients that are damaged when you heat your food. Cooking and processing destroys so many of the nutrients in your food because the chemical composition is actually altered by the heat.

If you use organic vegetables and fruit when you juice, you'll get even more benefit from your juicing. 6 to 8 servings of fruit and vegetables are recommended per day. In actuality, very few people actually reach that target.

You can juice both fruits and vegetables. However, remember

that fruits are high in natural sugars so if you have high blood pressure, deal with diabetes or are overweight, you might want to focus more on the vegetables than fruit.

The exception to that is lemon or lime, which have no sugars that can cause metabolic complications. They are also excellent with dark green vegetables because they eliminate the bitter taste

The Benefits of Juicing

There are three key reasons why you should consider making juicing part of your program for optimal health program:

1. **It allows you to eat a wider variety of vegetables in your diet.** Most of us put the same vegetables in our salads every day. That means we are not incorporating the principle of regular food rotation and it actually increases the likelihood of developing an allergy to a specific food. With juicing, you are able to juice a wide variety of vegetables that you might not always include in your diet.

2. **Juicing will help you absorb all the nutrients that vegetables have to offer.** The majority of us have impaired digestion because for many years most of us have made less-than-optimal food choices. Your body then becomes limited in its ability to absorb all the

vegetable nutrients that are available. Juicing helps you to "pre-digest" these nutrients, which allows you to get more nutrients from your vegetables.

3. **Juicing means you can consume an optimal amount of vegetables in an efficient manner.** You should eat one pound of raw vegetables for every 50 pounds of body weight per day. For many, eating that many vegetables is difficult, but with a quick glass of vegetable juice you can get there in no time.

Vegetable Juice is Not a Complete Meal

It is important to realize that vegetable juice has hardly any protein and no fat, so you can see that this is not a complete food. It needs to be used in addition to your regular meals not to replace them unless you are fasting. Ideally, you can consume your glass of juice as a snack or with your meal.

Tips to Help You Juice Healthy

#1 Use Pesticide Free Veggies

Whenever you can it is best to choose vegetables that you know are pesticide free. By doing so you allow yourself to get the optimum benefit from these veggies.

These vegetables are the worst for pesticides and should only be purchased if they are organic.

- Celery
- Spinach
- Kale
- Collard Greens
- Lettuce
- Carrots

#2 Start Juicing

This list is designed for those who are new to juicing. If you are pro already then you already have your own methods in place. However, you might still learn something.

Step 1: Start out with these vegetables, as they are the easiest to digest and tolerate:

- Celery
- Fennel (anise)
- Cucumbers

Step 2: Once you are used to juicing, you can start to add these vegetables:

- Endive

- Escarole
- Green leaf lettuce
- Red leaf lettuce
- Romaine lettuce
- Spinach

Cabbage juice is one of the most healing nutrients for ulcer repair as it is a huge source of vitamin U.

Step 3: When you're ready, you can begin to add herbs. Cilantro and parsley are both very nice. Be careful with cilantro as many don't tolerate it well. Start with a really small amount.

Step 4: The last step is to start to add the bitter greens. Add only a small amount at a time and use lime or lemon to remove the bitterness.
- Bitter Mustard Greens
- Collard Greens
- Dandelion Greens
- Kale

#3 Make Great Tasting Juice

If you want your juice to taste more palatable, you can add any of these elements:

- Lemons
- Limes
- Cranberries
- Fresh ginger

#4 Drink Your Vegetable Juice Immediately

Making your juice takes a great deal of time and so it's

 common to think that you'll just make up more and store it to consume later. The problem is that vegetable juice is very perishable and the nutrient value disappears rapidly, so it really is best to drink it right away.

If you store it in a sealed glass jar you can get 24 hours of storage out of it, with a lower loss of nutrients, but no longer. And it's still not recommended.

Fasting and Cleansing

We take baths and/or showers to keep the outside of our body clean, but we don't do a lot to keep the inside of our body clean, which is far more important. Even when you try to avoid eating toxic foods and drinks, drugs, environmental toxins, etc., you will still be getting toxins in your body due to the fact that your environment is polluted. Just recently, scientists found traces of rocket fuel inside the liver of polar bears that live in the middle of Alaska. That tells you pollution is everywhere and that not any of us are completely safe from it.

Thankfully, there is a way for you to remove toxins that have built up in your body over the years by "cleansing". You can choose from a number of different methods to cleanse your body, but fasting is thought to be one of the most natural methods.

When you fast you give your body a complete break from food, and since most of your energy goes into digesting the food that you eat, your body will suddenly have a way more free energy than normally and it will use this energy to work on internal things it would not normally have enough energy to address, such as removing built up toxins that may have been in your body for years.

Our bodies can heal itself from just about, but if the inside of your body is an extremely toxic environment diseases will be able to easily manifest and thrive. By fasting you give your body the best chance to do its work.

Different Types Of Fasting

There are many different types of fasting. Here we will briefly look at your different options.

1. Water Fasting

A **Water Fast** is where you consume only water for an extended period of time. This is by far the most powerful form of fasting, and it is generally not recommend unless you have a serious health problem. This type of fast should only be done under the supervision of an 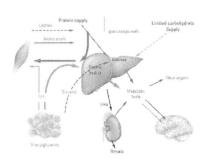 expert. The following two fasting methods are not as aggressive and are easier on your body.

2. Juice Fasting

A **Juice Fast** is a fast where you eat fruit and vegetable juices for an extended time period and you do not eat any sold foods.

This is a powerful internal cleanser. A juice fast is easier than a water fast because you will get calories and nutrition from the juice you drink. We will look at the juice fast in full detail in the next chapter.

3. Mono Fasting

A **Mono Fast** is the type of fast where you eat only one kind of fruit for an extended period of time.

While doing a Mono Fast you will still eat, but your digestive system still gets a huge break because you are eating simply and avoiding any food combinations.

Signs That You Are Toxic

Your body is a continuous state of detoxing and retoxing. Your body is designed to handle a fair amount of toxins every day, but you can take in toxins faster than they can be eliminated. For example, eating 3 toxic meals a day, drinking too much alcohol or smoking could be more toxins than your body can handle. In these cases you are headed for trouble, because if your body can't eliminate waste fast enough in time just about every health problem you can imagine will start to show up.

Let's look at some signs that you are toxic.

Your Urine
A healthy you, means your urine will be fairly clear. If your urine is dark yellow this can mean you are not drinking enough water to dilute the toxins or you are consuming too many toxins. Either way, going on a fast will help to flush you out your system.

Your Stool
What do animals in the wild, new born babies and the healthiest adults all have in common? Almost every time they eat they have a bowel movement. On average a person will eat around 100,000 pounds of food in their lifetime, which needs to be digested, so it's really important that your elimination is good. Some people are so constipated that they have only one or two bowel movement in a week. This is not healthy!

Your Body Odor

The best deodorant that you could have is clean living. When your body is healthy you don't have body odor. But an unhealthy body does have body odor.

Your Breath

If you wake up in the morning and your breath smells like the last night's dinner it means you haven't digested that meal. If this happens to you often, then fasting would be the best way to let your digestive system catch up and rejuvenate.

Your Skin

The health of your skin is a reflection of the health of your body on the inside. If you are prone to rashes, acne or skin conditions, it is usually the result of a poor diet. Your skin is your largest organ and it is replaced about once a month.

You shed about 1,000,000 dead skin cells every hour and almost all the dust in your home is actually your dead skin cells. Your skin has millions of pores, and we were built to sweat on a regular basis. You can sweat out toxins through exercise and you replace the toxic sweat by drinking clean water.

Your Health

Any time that you get sick, it you should fast until the sickness is over. It's 100% natural to stop eating when you are sick. It is natural for you to lose your appetite when you are sick and the reason for this is that your body is being attacked by a virus and your body is trying to fight it off and get rid of it before it takes over your body, so the last thing needed is for energy to be used to digest food.

Warning

If you have spent the past number of years eating too much unhealthy food, drinks, taking drugs, and/or breathing polluted air, you are likely full of toxins and there is a very good chance that if you fast you will experience something called a "Healing Crisis," which is when so many toxins are being removed from your body that you develop symptoms of sickness.

Your body has 7 organs that are designed to eliminate toxins. They are the liver, colon, kidneys, blood, lungs, lymphatic System, and skin. When massive quantities of toxins are being eliminated from your body these organs will be working very hard, and when this happens the following things can occur:

- You find you suddenly need to use the bathroom way more than normal.
- You get really bad breath
- You develop body odor
- You develop skin problems
- You go through intense mood swings
- You feel old injuries that you had suffered a long time ago – they flare up and hurt again
- You start thinking about the memories you have suppressed for years.
- You feel weak and tired and want to stay in bed
- You start losing weight
- Your hands and feet feel cold
- You develop flu-like symptoms
- You develop a temporary white coloring on your tongue
- When you stand up you feel dizzy
- You have pain around your joints
- You can't stop thinking about unhealthy foods

You might think that something is seriously wrong, but in most cases this actually indicates that the fast is working. Your body is cleaning house.

Ending Your Fast

When you fast, you need to be careful about what you choose to eat when your fast ends. During your fast your stomach will  shrink and your metabolism will slow way down. This is why when you end your fast it is you need to slowly reintroduce food to your body. Your first meal should be very small, and each meal can get a little bigger until you can eat a regular size meal comfortably.

Food Allergies

Food allergies aren't that common, but they can be very serious. Only 3 percent of adults have food allergies that have been clinically proven. Food allergies are different from food intolerances, which are quite common. Food allergies are usually different between children and adults. Children can outgrow their allergies, but adults tend to have them forever. Once you are diagnosed with a food allergy, generally the treatment is simply to not eat that food(s).

The Signs and Symptoms of Food Allergies

Digestion is a complex process, but food allergy symptoms occur within a few minutes to an hour of eating the food. A food allergy can start with itching in the mouth and it can quickly become difficult to swallow and breathe.

During digestion of the food in the stomach and intestines, you might experience vomiting, nausea, diarrhea and abdominal pain. Allergy symptoms that occur in the stomach and intestines are commonly confused with the symptoms of different types of food intolerance.

The allergens are absorbed and enter your bloodstream. Once they reach the skin these allergens can cause eczema and hives. When they reach the airways, they can cause asthma. As they travel through your bloodstream, the can cause weakness, light-headedness an in the worst cases anaphylaxis.

The Most Common Food Allergies

In adults, the most common foods that cause allergies are:

- Eggs
- Fish
- Legume
- Nuts from trees (i.e. walnuts)
- Peanuts
- Shellfish (i.e. shrimp, lobster, crayfish, crab)

If you are highly allergic to a food, even a minuscule amount of a food allergen can evoke an allergic reaction. If you are less sensitive you might be able to tolerate small amounts of the food they are allergic to.

Cross-reactivity, which occurs when an allergic reaction occurs o foods that are chemically or otherwise related to a food you are directly related to. If you have a life threatening allergy to a specific food, you will almost always be told to avoid all related foods. For example, if you have a history of having a serious allergic reaction to crab, you should avoid lobster, shrimp and all shellfish.

Be Careful Allergies

If you think you have a food allergy it is important for you to establish that to be true and what the severity of that allergy is. Too often we don't take these things overly seriously, especially if the symptoms are not too severe, but the trouble is those symptoms can change and suddenly you can have a life threatening condition, so take your food allergies seriously and make sure you know your risks.

Conclusion

We're happy to see you here at the end. By now you have learned a lot about healthy, holistic nutrition that's practical and easy to make a part of your day-to-day life.

Our ancestors ate healthier than we did, for many reasons. They ate foods that were grown locally and often without the use of pesticides and they did not have access to the processed foods we are surrounded with.

Sure, there's no question that those processed foods are

convenient and make life easier, but at what risk. It's very likely that at some point that convenience is going to negatively affect your health.

What's great is that now you have all the tools you need to eat a healthy diet, you have all kinds of practical nutrition and your fingertips and before you know it, you'll be putting together healthy meals in less time than it takes to go to the store and buy something prepackaged and processed.

Congratulations on making the decision to take control of your

health and to help your body become

healthier through holistic, practical

eating. Your well on your way to

becoming a healthier you!

Made in the USA
San Bernardino, CA
29 December 2016